Contents

Some words are shown in bold, **like this**. You can
find out what they mean by looking in the glossary.

What is a life cycle?

All living things, from tiny insects to tall trees, have a life cycle. Some life cycles can last for just a few days, and others can go on for thousands of years. A living **organism** can begin life in many different ways. It may, as with humans, be born. Some living things hatch from eggs, and others sprout from **seeds**. A few organisms, such as hydra, start life when they grow on a part of their parent's body.

Once an organism begins its life, it grows and changes. In time, it will be ready to make its own young. It may lay eggs, produce seeds or give birth. Some living things produce young only once before they die. Others can go on **reproducing** for years. In the end, living things will die. They may be killed by a **predator**, or die of illness or old age. Often, their offspring survive to continue the life cycle.

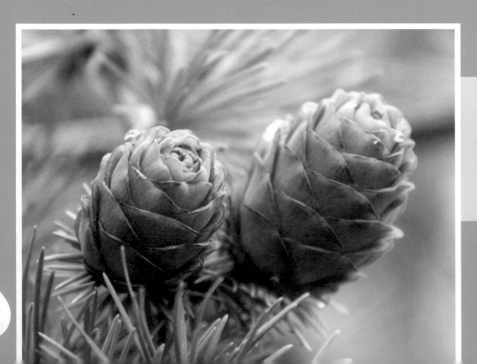

The pine cones on this tree each contain many small seeds, which can grow into new trees.

Life Cycles

Nancy Dickmann

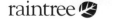

raintree

a Capstone company — publishers for children

Raintree is an imprint of Capstone Global Library Limited, a company incorporated in England and Wales having its registered office at 264 Banbury Road, Oxford, OX2 7DY – Registered company number: 6695582

www.raintree.co.uk
myorders@raintree.co.uk

Produced for Raintree by Calcium
Editors: Sarah Eason and Harriet McGregor
Designer: Paul Myerscough
Originated by Capstone Global Library Limited © 2018
Printed and bound in India

ISBN 978 1 4747 6537 4
22 21 20 19 18
10 9 8 7 6 5 4 3 2 1

British Library Cataloguing in Publication Data
A full catalogue record for this book is available from the British Library.

Acknowledgements
Picture credits: Cover: Shutterstock: Alex James Bramwell; Insides: Shutterstock: Chris Alcock 26–27, Nick Biemans 29b, Bluedogroom 4–5, David Evison 1, 18–19, Eric Gevaert 20–21, Inlovepai 8–9, Brian A. Jackson 6t, Sebastian Kaulitzki 15b, Kkaplin 10–11, Leungchopan 12–13, Monkey Business Images 13tr, 14–15, Krzysztof Odziomek 27t, Paladin12 6–7, PCHT 21b, Rawpixel 16, Villiers Steyn 23, Taiftin 4, TessarTheTegu 24–25, Tulpahn 9t, Dennis van de Water 28–29, Wildnerdpix 11, K.A.Willis 18b, Roger Wissmann 22, Matej Ziak 25b, ZouZou 16–17.

Every effort has been made to contact copyright holders of material reproduced in this book. Any omissions will be rectified in subsequent printings if notice is given to the publisher.

All the internet addresses (URLs) given in this book were valid at the time of going to press. However, due to the dynamic nature of the internet, some addresses may have changed, or sites may have changed or ceased to exist since publication. While the author and publisher regret any inconvenience this may cause readers, no responsibility for any such changes can be accepted by either the author or the publisher.

During their life cycle, most living things carry out life processes. For example, all living things grow. They must take in and use food, and get rid of waste. They also reproduce, which means making more living things of the same type.

After hatching, this baby snake will grow and develop until it is able to lay its own eggs.

How plants grow

The life cycle of many types of plants starts with a seed. A seed contains the beginnings of a new plant. It also has food that the new plant will need. When a seed absorbs water, the process of sprouting begins. The outer seed case splits, and roots develop. The roots extend into the soil and take up water and **nutrients**.

Seeds can travel away from their parent plant in different ways. These dandelion seeds are very light and shaped so that they can blow on the wind.

The first shoots and leaves grow upwards, and use sunlight to make food for the plant. More and more leaves grow, and the plant gets taller and thicker. Once it is grown, it will be ready to make its own seeds.

Some types of plants do not grow from seeds. For example, a potato produces tiny sprouts. If these are cut off and planted, they will grow into new potatoes. A strawberry plant sends out special stems called "runners" across the ground. These runners work their way into the ground and form roots for new plants.

Plants need water, air, sunlight, warmth and nutrients in order to grow. Plants combine the energy from sunlight with water and gases in the air to make their own food. This process is called **photosynthesis**. Water is also needed to keep plant stems strong.

These seedlings have sprouted from seeds beneath the surface of the soil. Once the store of food inside the seeds is used up, the seeds will break up and disappear.

Flowers, fruit and pollination

The life cycle continues when a full-grown plant makes its own seeds. Many plants have flowers with both male and female parts. The male parts produce **pollen**, which is like sticky dust. To make seeds, the pollen must be transferred to the female parts of a plant.

Pollen can be blown from one plant to another by the wind. But many plants rely on insects, birds and bats to spread their pollen. Their flowers produce a sweet liquid called nectar. When animals come to the flower to drink the nectar, they brush against the male parts, and pollen sticks to their bodies. When they fly to another plant, the pollen brushes onto its female parts. Once this happens, the flower can make seeds. Often the seeds develop inside a fruit such as an apple.

EARTH BY NUMBERS

Plants have different ways of attracting insects, birds and other pollinators. They provide a "reward" in the form of nectar or pollen to eat. Some animals are attracted by a flower's bright colours. Others may like its scent – even if it smells disgusting to humans! Some flowers are specially shaped to form a landing platform for flying insects.

Nectar is an important food for bees, butterflies and many other animals. Nectar is sugary and full of energy.

Some seeds are spread when an animal eats a plant's fruit. The seeds come out later in their waste.

PLANT LIFE CYCLES—BY NUMBERS!

Many scientists believe that the oldest living individual plant is a bristlecone pine tree in the United States, that is

5,065

years old.

A type of palm called the Coco-de-mer produces the largest seeds of any plant. They can be almost

50

centimetres (20 inches) across and weigh as much as 30 kilograms (66 pounds)!

The record for the largest single flower belongs to the *Rafflesia arnoldii*, which produces flowers that are up to

91

centimetres (3 feet) across and weigh up to 7 kilograms (15 pounds). The *Titan arum* plant produces enormous clusters of tiny flowers, which can be 3.5 metres (12 feet) high and weigh as much as 77 kg (170 pounds)!

The tallest type of tree on Earth is the coastal redwood, found on the west coast of the United States. The tallest one ever found was

115

metres (379 feet) tall. That's as tall as a 35-storey building!

A seed can stay dormant for a long time before sprouting. Scientists believe that the oldest seed ever to sprout was

1,288

years old.

An avocado has just one seed. Most apples have between 2 and 15 seeds. A single strawberry has about

200

seeds.

Human life cycles

A human baby starts with the joining of two **cells** inside the mother. During the nine months that it stays in the **uterus**, it grows and changes. Its organs and other body parts develop. When the baby is born, it is helpless. During childhood, a baby grows and learns. By the time it is 12 years old, a child will weigh more than 10 times its birth weight. He or she will be able to speak, read, write and do complex tasks.

Around the age of 12, boys and girls go through a phase called puberty. This is the stage when a child's body changes to be more like an adult. Inside the body, changes are happening to make it possible to have children.

During adulthood, humans stop growing, and many of them have their own children. In old age, some body parts no longer work as well as they used to. Eventually, all humans will die.

EARTH BY NUMBERS

Your body is made up of tiny building blocks called cells. Many of these cells are constantly dying and being replaced by new ones. Cells lining your stomach may live only for a few days, while skin cells may last for a month. Some cells, such as nerve cells, last a lifetime.

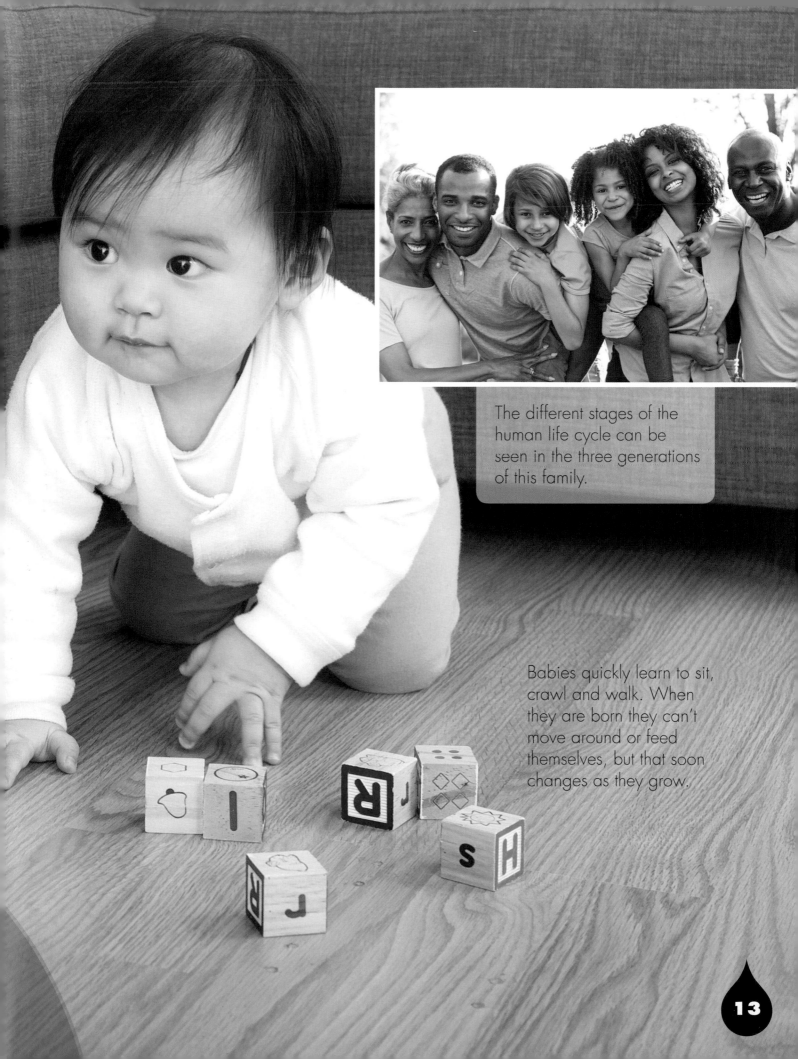

The different stages of the human life cycle can be seen in the three generations of this family.

Babies quickly learn to sit, crawl and walk. When they are born they can't move around or feed themselves, but that soon changes as they grow.

Human reproduction

A woman's body contains special cells called eggs, and a man produces cells called sperm. When an egg and a sperm join, an **embryo** is formed. This tiny clump of cells attaches to the wall of the woman's uterus. Then it begins to grow and develop. The cells divide to form new cells, and soon the cells start to specialize. For example, some will become blood cells, some will be bone cells and some will be skin cells.

After about three weeks, the embryo's heart begins to pump blood. By the time the embryo is 10 weeks old, nearly all of its organs are completely formed. At this stage, it is called a **fetus**. Within another few weeks, the fingers and toes are formed. The fetus continues to grow and develop. After about nine months inside the mother's body, it is born.

A child may get its father's hair colour and its mother's eye colour.

EARTH BY NUMBERS

Every person has many different physical **traits**: for example, they may be tall, with brown hair and blue eyes, and be right-handed. These traits are controlled by the **genes** that have been passed down by the person's parents. A child has a mixture of genes from both parents, so their traits are usually a mixture, too.

During the time that a baby is in the uterus, it gets everything it needs, including food and oxygen, from its mother.

15

HUMANS—BY NUMBERS!

The oldest person that ever lived was a Frenchwoman called Jeanne Calment. She died in 1997 at the age of **122**.

The most common hair colour in the world is black, and the most common eye colour is brown. Only around **1–2** per cent of the world's population has red hair, and about 2 per cent has green eyes.

Between **5** per cent and **30** per cent of people are left-handed.

In the United States in 1911, the average number of children a woman would have during her life was 3.4. By 2011, that had dropped to 1.9 children per woman.

Although men can father children at any age, most women find it difficult to become pregnant after the age of around 45. The average age of a woman having her first child in England and Wales is 28.6 years. The oldest known mother in the world was nearly 67 years old when she gave birth to twin boys.

The human life cycle begins when two cells merge. Scientists believe that there are around 37.2 trillion cells in an adult human body.

Animal reproduction

Humans are **mammals**, and many other mammals reproduce in a similar way. One or more fetuses grow in the mother's uterus until they are ready to be born. Some mammals, such as cats, are pregnant for a shorter time and have more babies. Others, such as elephants, are pregnant for longer.

Some other animals produce young in completely different ways. Birds lay eggs and then sit on them until they are ready to hatch. Inside the egg, a baby bird slowly takes shape. Many reptiles also lay eggs, although most of them do not take care of the eggs. Nearly all amphibians, and some types of fish, also lay eggs.

A sea turtle lays up to 200 eggs in the sand, then returns to the sea, leaving the eggs behind. When they hatch, the babies must make their own way to the water.

A newborn kangaroo is small and not well-developed. It climbs into its mother's pouch to drink milk and grow for several more months.

Some animals, including humans and elephants, usually give birth to a single baby at a time. Others, such as mice or fish, might give birth to many young, often several times in one year. Animals that have fewer babies can take care of them and keep them safe until they are ready to survive on their own. Animals that have many offspring cannot raise them as carefully. Many of the young will die, but at least a few will survive to continue the life cycle.

Raising young

A human child often lives with its parents for 18 years or more. It depends on its parents for food and shelter. In the animal kingdom, this is very unusual. Many baby animals have to take care of themselves, and very few stay with their parents for more than a few years.

In some species, such as penguins, the mother and father work together to care for the babies. Other animal mothers, such as polar bears, must do it by themselves. Some types of animals, such as lions and elephants, live in groups. All the adult females in a group will help take care of the babies.

Animal parents have many different ways of keeping their animals safe and travelling with them. Some fish carry their babies in their mouths. Wolf spiders carry several tiny spiderlings on their backs. Many baby monkeys use their strong fingers to cling to their mother's fur.

EARTH BY NUMBERS

Animal parents often find food for their young, and some parents actually produce it. All female mammals have mammary glands, which produce milk.

The milk contains fat, protein, sugars and other nutrients that the baby needs. The baby drinks milk until its body is ready to digest other types of food.

A young orangutan depends on its mother for food and to get around for the first two years of its life.

These baby sun birds will be brought food by their parents until they are big enough to take care of themselves.

ANIMAL LIFE CYCLES—BY NUMBERS!

Some animals live an incredibly long time. One giant tortoise was thought to be 250 years old when it died. Scientists believe that a type of reptile called the tuatara can live for more than 200 years.

A termite queen can lay 30,000 eggs in a single day, and about 250 million eggs in her lifetime. But that's nothing compared to the ocean sunfish, which can produce 300 million eggs at a time!

The vervain hummingbird lays the smallest egg of any bird species. The egg is less than 1 centimetre (0.39 inches) long and weighs 0.36 grams (0.0128 ounces). The biggest egg belongs to the ostrich. It can weigh more than 2.3 kg (5 pounds).

The African elephant stays pregnant for longer than any other mammal: about

22

months. The mammal with the shortest pregnancy is the Virginia opossum, at just 12 or 13 days.

Most of the milk we drink comes from cows. A dairy cow can produce around

30 litres

(8 gallons) of milk each day.

The egg of a kiwi bird can weigh up to

25 per cent of the

mother's body weight. If a human baby was this big when it was born, it would be like giving birth to a four-year-old child!

Metamorphosis

Kittens and puppies look a lot like their parents. Some types of baby animals – including many insects – look completely different from their parents. Their bodies must go through a process called **metamorphosis** before they become adults.

Many insects are shaped a bit like worms or caterpillars when they hatch from eggs. This stage in the life cycle is called a **larva**. The larva eats and grows and, sometimes, it sheds its stiff outer skin if the skin gets too small. Once a larva is big enough, it enters a new stage and is called a **pupa**. During this stage the insect does not eat or move around. Its body is protected by a skin or cocoon while it changes shape. After a while, an adult insect emerges.

EARTH BY NUMBERS

Insects are a well-known example of metamorphosis, but other types of animals also go through this process. Frogs start life as fish-like tadpoles, living in water and eating algae. Eventually their bodies change, and they begin a new life on land, eating insects. Some sea creatures, such as shrimp and lobsters, also go through metamorphosis.

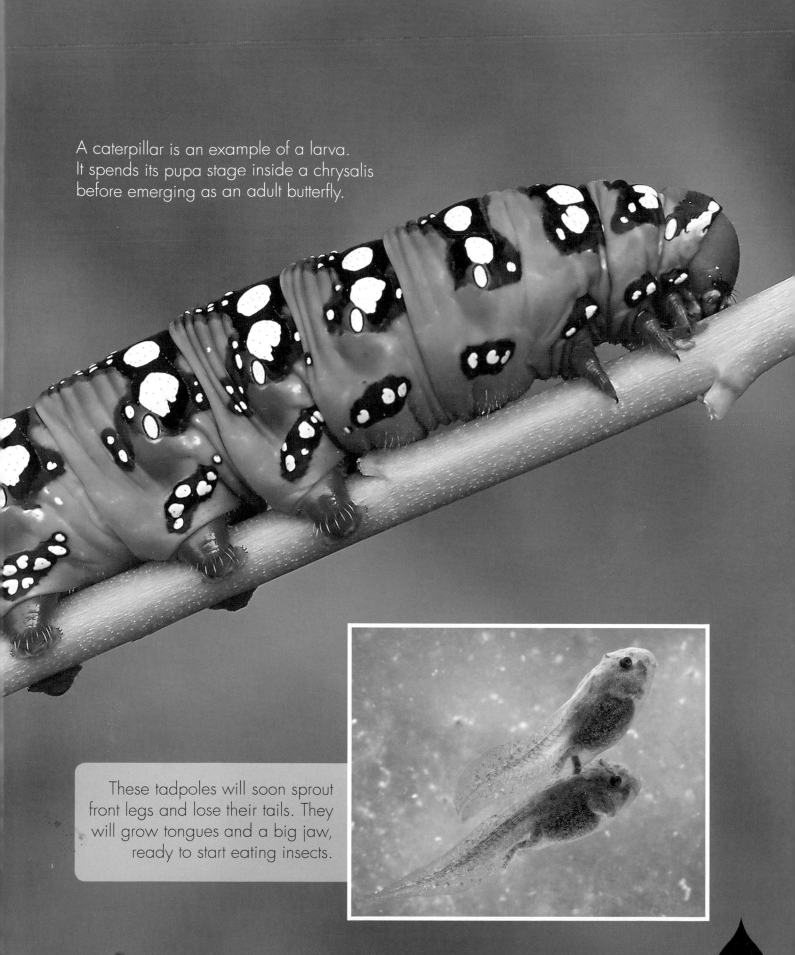

A caterpillar is an example of a larva. It spends its pupa stage inside a chrysalis before emerging as an adult butterfly.

These tadpoles will soon sprout front legs and lose their tails. They will grow tongues and a big jaw, ready to start eating insects.

Unusual life cycles

In the animal kingdom, there are some weird and wonderful life cycles. Clownfish begin their life as males, but some become females as they grow older. Other types of fish can change from female to male. Eels change their **habitat**, not their sex. As young eels they live in freshwater rivers, but they swim to the salt water of the ocean to give birth.

The periodical cicadas of the eastern United States are the longest-living insect on the continent. When these insects hatch from their eggs, the white, ant-like young dig into the soil. They stay underground for years, sucking liquid from the roots of plants. They grow and develop until one day, the adult cicadas all emerge creating a noisy flying swarm.

Some cicada species stay underground for 13 years, and others stay underground for 17 years.

EARTH BY NUMBERS

One of the most amazing animals of all is the immortal jellyfish. Scientists recently discovered that these jellyfish can reverse their life cycles. All jellyfish start as a small blob (called a polyp) before taking their adult shape. Incredibly, the immortal jellyfish can change back into a polyp when it is starving or under stress. Then it slowly grows back into an adult jellyfish – and it can do this again and again.

Orange-and-white striped clownfish live on many coral reefs.

Life cycles on Earth

There are many different animals and plants on Earth, and they all have different life cycles. From seeds sprouting to eggs hatching, there are a lot of ways for living things to grow and reproduce.

Everything lives in a habitat, which could be a dry desert, a cold ocean or even a rotting tree in a forest. Many plant and animal life cycles have developed in order to **adapt** to a habitat. For example, some cacti are able to grow very quickly. When conditions are good, they shoot up fast.

Many animals, such as bears, **hibernate** during the winter. Food is hard to find then, so by hibernating the bears use less energy. Many mother bears give birth during the hibernation period, waking up every now and then to feed or clean their cubs.

Everywhere you look, you can see life cycles in action.

EARTH BY NUMBERS

Many plants and animals never get to complete their life cycle. They may be eaten by a predator, or cut down for food. Humans can affect the life cycles of plants and animals.

When we build towns and clear land for farming, we destroy or change habitats. The plants and animals that live there must adapt or move to a new habitat in order to survive.

This zebra's life cycle has been cut short, but the mother lion is teaching her cubs how to hunt and survive on their own.

Glossary

adapt change, over time, in order to survive and reproduce in a particular habitat

cells smallest building blocks of life. Plants and animals are made up of cells.

embryo animal that is just starting to develop inside its mother, or inside an egg or seed

fetus unborn baby that is more developed than an embryo. A human baby is called a fetus once it has been growing for about two months.

genes codes inside a cell that cause particular traits, such as hair colour. Genes are passed down from parents to offspring.

habitat natural environment of an animal or plant

hibernate sleep through the winter in a den or burrow to save energy

larva young form of some types of insect, before it changes into an adult. Larvae do not have wings and they look a bit like worms.

mammals group of animals that have fur or hair and that make milk to feed their babies

metamorphosis change in shape of some living things as they grow. A caterpillar changing into a butterfly is an example of metamorphosis.

nutrients substances in food that a living thing needs in order to grow and stay healthy

organism living thing

photosynthesis process in which a plant uses sunlight to change water and carbon dioxide into food for itself

pollen sticky powder made by flowers that helps them to form seeds

predator animal that hunts other animals for food

pupa middle stage of some insect life cycles. Some insects spend their time as a pupa inside a cocoon.

reproducing having babies (offspring)

seeds small parts of a flowering plant that grow into new plants

traits characteristics that make a living thing different from others of the same type, for example, height or eye colour

uterus sac-like organ inside a female mammal in which a fetus develops

Find out more

Books

Human Body: A Children's Encyclopedia (DK Reference), DK
(DK Children, 2012)

Inheritance of Traits: Why is My Dog Bigger Than Your Dog? (Show Me Science),
Jen Green (Raintree, 2015)

Life Cycles (Life Science Stories), Angela Royston (Raintree, 2017)

Life Processes (Essential Life Science), Richard and Louise Spilsbury
(Raintree, 2013)

Plant Reproduction: How Do You Grow a Giant Pumpkin? (Show Me Science),
Cath Senker (Raintree, 2015)

Websites

Discover more about the life cycles of different organisms at:
www.bbc.co.uk/education/clips/zwrn2p3

Find out more about the life cycle of humans at:
www.dkfindout.com/uk/human-body/life-cycle

Watch this video of a plant's life cycle:
www.dkfindout.com/uk/video/animals-and-nature/life-cycle-plant-video

Index